PLANET FOOTBALL

CROATIA

GREATEST FANS

CONTENTS

Published in paperback
in 2017 by Wayland
Copyright © Hodder and
Stoughton, 2017
All rights reserved

Editor: Victoria Brooker
Produced for Wayland by
Tall Tree Ltd
Designer: Gary Hyde
Editor: Jon Richards
Dewey number: 796.3'34-dc23

ISBN 978 1 5263 0359 2

Wayland, an imprint of
Hachette Children's Group
Part of Hodder and Stoughton
Carmelite House
50 Victoria Embankment
London EC4Y 0DZ
An Hachette UK Company
www.hachette.co.uk
www.hachettechildrens.co.uk

FSC

Printed and bound in China
10 9 8 7 6 5 4 3 2 1

FANATICS!

Football is the most played and enjoyed team sport in the world. FIFA – the organisation that runs world football – estimates that as many as 220 million people regularly play the sport. Even more are football fans who watch games live, on TV or via the Internet.

More than 10 million people went to games in Spain's La Liga in the 2014–15 season, while over 5.25 million fans turned up to watch the 18 teams take part in Japan's J-League matches in 2014. Millions more support their local clubs in the lower leagues, experiencing the highs and lows of wins and defeats and the excitement and drama of the game.

GUANGZHOU FANS

ARGENTINA FANS

Argentina fans watch sadly as their team loses the final of the 2014 World Cup against Germany. Fans get upset at a bad defeat, but quickly look forward to the next game as there is always hope of a memorable victory in the future.

EVER

Football has an incredible grip over many supporters. They attend as many games as they can and spend much of their spare time debating team news, who their side should buy and play and other football matters. Some name their pets or children after their favourite players. These people really are football crazy!

As well as following their favourite club, many people, such as these Polish fans, watch their country's team as it takes part in international competitions, such as the FIFA World Cup.

POLISH FANS

广州恒大

EVERGRANDE

广州队

Fans of Chinese club Guangzhou Evergrande celebrate as their club wins its first-ever AFC Champions League competition in 2013 – the biggest prize in Asian club football. More than 42,000 fans came to each one of their games in the 2014 Chinese league season.

"THE SUPPORTERS ARE THE LIFEBLOOD OF PROFESSIONAL FOOTBALL – THEY ARE THE IDENTITY OF THE CLUBS. OWNERS, COACHES AND PLAYERS CHANGE BUT SUPPORTERS ALWAYS REMAIN."
UEFA PRESIDENT, MICHEL PLATINI

KITTED OUT

Most fans like to say it loud and proud by wearing their football team's shirts and other items – from wigs to gloves – in their team colours. Fans are passionate about these colours. It is part of the identity of the club or national team they support.

Many famous clubs today play in different coloured kits to those of the past. Liverpool, famous for playing in red today, used to play in blue and white, while the black and white stripes of Juventus came after the Italian club's original bright pink shirts.

EURO 2012

Ireland fans in green mix with Croatia fans wearing their distinctive red and white squared shirts at Euro 2012. The Irish fans were awarded the best fans of the tournament by UEFA.

NUMBERS GAME

1,580,000

The number of replica shirts, Spanish club Real Madrid sold in the 2013–14 season.

A collection of Barcelona shirts are on display at the Spanish club's giant megastore at their Camp Nou stadium. In 2014, more than 2 million people visited the store, many buying replica shirts.

Club shops sell thousands of replica shirts each year. Turkish club, Fenerbahce sold 325,000 shirts in 2014, while Italian league champions, Juventus sold 375,000 and Bayern Munich a staggering 945,000. Most top clubs change their kit design each season and some fans insist on buying the latest kit each year.

SWEDISH FANS

Lively fans of the Swedish national team wear yellow and blue shirts, wigs and facepaint at the 2012 European Championships. Swedish fans are well known for their passion and good humour.

HOME AND AWAY

Football clubs in a league play half of their matches at their home stadium and the rest at other team's grounds. Some fans travel long distances to offer their support when their team plays away.

Many club fans buy a season ticket which gives them access to all their team's home games. These vary wildly in price even among the top leagues of the world. In Germany, an adult season ticket at Bayern Munich can cost less than £150, while at Arsenal, season tickets can cost more than £2,000.

PORTUGAL

For fans of major Portuguese teams, Benfica and Sporting Lisbon, an away game at their rivals doesn't involve a great deal of travel as their two grounds are just 3 km apart.

Club Deportivo Guadalajara fans wait patiently in a long queue for tickets at the Omnilife Stadium in Mexico. Demand for tickets for a crucial big match can be huge and priority is often given to season ticket holders first.

MEXICO

Going to away games can be an exciting experience for fans, but also an expensive and time-consuming one. It can involve hours on the road, on trains or in the air. Once they have arrived at the ground, away fans are often directed to a dedicated area of the stadium to sit, separated from the home fans.

BELGIUM

These Belgian fans dressed as devils have travelled more than 9,000 km to attend the 2014 World Cup in Brazil. At major tournaments, like the World Cup, foreign fans tend to be given a very warm welcome with stewards employed by the hosts who speak their language.

"THE SAMPDORIA FANS APPLAUDED ME AFTER WE SCORED... THE STEWARDS OFFERED ME COFFEE... COMPLIMENTING ME ON MY PASSION." UDINESE FAN, ARRIGO BROVEDANI WHO ARRIVED FOR AN ITALIAN SERIE A GAME IN 2012 TO DISCOVER HE WAS THE ONLY AWAY FAN IN THE GROUND!

9

THE MATCH DAY

Every fan's matchday experience may be slightly different. However, they all start with the trip to the ground, perhaps meeting friends outside, and then heading into the stadium as the atmosphere builds before kick-off.

Fans may buy drink, food or matchday programmes at the ground. But if they visited Swiss club FC Sion in 2014, they were served a free dish of raclette – a hot meal of cheese and potatoes! Some clubs also put on pre-match entertainment, such as bands, before an explosion of noise greets the two teams coming out of the players' tunnel onto the pitch.

EURO 2012 FANZONE

Fans enjoy the big game atmosphere at a Euro 2012 fanzone. These are built at major tournaments and contain food and drink stalls, entertainment stages and giant screens, which display match action for fans without tickets.

During the match, a stadium can be transformed into a noisy riot of colour as scarves and banners are waved. Fans of Uruguayan team, Penarol, unveiled the world's biggest football banner in 2011. It measured over 48 m high and needed 300 fans just to carry it to the ground!

SOUTH AFRICA

In South African football, noise can be ear-splitting due to the vuvuzuela – a plastic trumpet-like horn which became very popular with fans of all teams at the 2010 World Cup.

NUMBERS GAME

80,423

The average number of fans who went to every 2014–15 league game of German club, Borussia Dortmund.

ATHLETIC BILBAO

Bilbao fans congregate outside Barcelona's Nou Camp before the final of the 2015 Copa del Rey. Stewards inside the ground direct fans to their seats and prevent crowd problems such as pitch invasions.

"WHEN YOU START SUPPORTING A FOOTBALL CLUB, YOU DON'T SUPPORT IT BECAUSE OF THE TROPHIES, OR A PLAYER, OR HISTORY, YOU SUPPORT IT BECAUSE YOU... FOUND A PLACE WHERE YOU BELONG."
DUTCH FOOTBALLER, DENNIS BERGKAMP

SUPERSTITIONS & TRADITIONS

Some fans have unusual superstitions, such as wearing an item of lucky clothing to the match. Here are some fun fan traditions and actions performed at matches.

The first Mexican waves weren't Mexican but American, performed by American Football crowds at the start of the 1980s. The move got its name and worldwide popularity, though, when it was performed by football fans at the 1986 World Cup held in Mexico.

Spain's superfan bangs his drum and urges the crowd on. Known as 'Manolo el del bombo', Manuel Cáceres Artesero is found among Spain fans at every national team game, and has only missed one match since 1982.

MANOLO EL DEL BOMBO

Two unusual traditions occur in football stadiums after games have finished. Japanese fans have a tradition of picking up litter after a match, leaving their part of a football stadium clean. Around 20,000 fans of German club, FC Union Berlin, come to their ground every Christmas Eve to sing carols.

POLISH FANS

LECH POZNAN FANS

Another crowd move is named after Polish football club, Lech Poznan and is thought to have begun in the 1960s. When a goal is scored, the fans turn their back on the pitch, link arms and jump up and down.

"WE TRY TO DO A LITTLE BIT OF A CLEAN-UP TO SHOW RESPECT TO THE HOST COUNTRY AND SHOW OFF HOW CLEAN THINGS ARE IN JAPAN."
KEI KAWAI, JAPANESE FOOTBALL FAN AT THE 2014 WORLD CUP

MAD MASCOTS

Many clubs have some form of mascot that often parades around a football ground before the game. The mascot poses for photos, urges the crowd to encourage their team and, away from the match, is used in promoting the club and to support local charities.

The first mascots were real animals. These included a St Bernard dog for Newton Heath in the 1900s (before the club changed its name to Manchester United) and Cologne's Hennes the goat who appeared in team photos alongside the footballers from 1950 onwards. Most mascots today are cuddly animals or fantasy characters with a person inside who meets and greets the fans.

FERENCVÁROS EAGLE

The person inside the Fradi Eagle – mascot of Hungarian club, Ferencváros – takes a rest before a match. At some clubs, people inside the mascot are volunteers. At others, they are paid employees of the club.

14

Milanello became Italian club AC Milan's new mascot in 2006. The mascot was designed to look like a little devil by famous cartoon film makers, Warner Brothers, and is named after the club's training ground.

AC MILAN'S DEVIL

WILSA KRAKOW DRAGON

The Wawel Dragon is the official mascot of Polish club, Wisla Krakow. They play in Poland's top division, the Ekstraklasa, and have won the league title 14 times.

COMPETITION MASCOTS

Many major football competitions have their own mascot or mascots. These are unveiled several years before the tournament and are used to publicise the event in advance.

GOLEO

The first FIFA World Cup was held in 1930, but it wasn't until the 1966 World Cup in England that a tournament had a mascot – a lion wearing the national flag as a shirt called World Cup Willie. Since then, mascots have included a chilli pepper called Pique at Mexico in 1986 and Footix the cockerel at France 1998.

Goleo – a lion wearing an old-style German football shirt – was the mascot of the 2006 World Cup held in Germany. He was built by the company who made the Muppets and Sesame Street puppet characters.

SLAVEK AND SLAVKO

Euro 2012 was jointly held in Poland and the Ukraine, so the tournament had two mascots, Slavek in Polish colours (on the left) and Slavko in Ukraine's (on the right).

Other competitions, beside the World Cup, have got in on the action with their own mascots. The 2015 African Cup of Nations, for example, had a porcupine named Chuku Chuku. The 2015 Copa Libertadores in Chile had a red fox whose name, Zincha, was chosen by the public following an internet vote. Zincha even had its own Twitter account.

ZAKUMI

Styled on a leopard, an animal found in South Africa, with a shock of green hair, Zakumi was the mascot for the 2010 World Cup. Its name comes from ZA, the letters for South Africa, and the word 'kumi', meaning 'ten', for the year of the tournament.

FULECO

NUMBERS GAME

47

The number of different designs from which Fuleco was chosen by the organisers of the 2014 FIFA World Cup.

Fuleco was the mascot of the 2014 World Cup in Brazil. Fuleco was designed as a three-banded armadillo, a creature found in Brazil.

DERBY GAMES

Derby matches are passionate games between two rival clubs. Some have a long history such as Penarol and Nacional contesting derby games in Uruguay since 1900. For many fans, these are the most eagerly anticipated matches of the season.

Most club rivalries come from the two sides being neighbours. Many cities around the world have two leading teams which compete for supremacy. These include Roma and Lazio in the Italian city of Rome, Celtic and Rangers in Glasgow, Fenerbahce and Galatasaray in Istanbul, Flamengo and Fluminense in Rio de Janeiro and Al-Ahly and Zamalek in the Cairo derby in Egypt.

MILAN VS INTER

Devoted AC Milan fans put on a colourful display before the Milan derby match against Internazionale. Inter have won 76 of the 213 official derbies between the two teams, just two wins ahead of AC Milan.

One of the biggest derbies in South America pits Boca Juniors and River Plate against each other. The Boca fans call their opponents 'gallinas' (meaning 'chickens'), while the River Plate fans call their rivals 'los puercos' (meaning 'pigs'). Charming!

BOCA JUNIORS

Sometimes, the rivalry extends well beyond city limits. Teams like Paris Saint-Germain and Marseilles in France and the Mexican sides of Chivas and Clube America are each based in separate cities. The Barcelona v Real Madrid derby in Spain, known as 'El Clásico', is watched with interest by the entire country.

BARCA V REAL

Barca and Real Madrid fans mingle before a derby match hoping for plenty of goals, as 988 have been scored in El Clásico derbies up until August 2015.

"I DON'T WANT ANY CUPS, I DON'T WANT TO BE A CHAMPION EITHER, I'VE GOT TWO WISHES, TWO WISHES TO BEAT FENER."
A POPULAR CHANT OF GALATASARAY FANS WHEN THEY PLAY FENERBAHCE

SPORTING SOUVENIRS

For many fans, owning a replica shirt of the team they support is not enough. To show their allegiance and loyalty, they want lots of items branded in their team's colours. Clubs and national teams are happy to sell them all sorts of merchandise to make a profit.

ITALY

Merchandise bought by fans ranges from pens, aprons, bags and bathroom rubber ducks in team colours to slippers which make a crowd noise every time a fan takes a step. These and hundreds of other items are sold at a club's shop or online over the Internet.

An official shop in Milan sells football shirts and other merchandise. In 2014, rivals AC Milan and Internazionale sold approximately 775,000 shirts between them – a staggering number.

105.2

The number of millions of Euros, German club Bayern Munich, made in 2014 from sales of merchandise including scarfs and clothing.

SOLDADO
SILVA
KUN AGUERO
DZEKO
WILSHERE
S.CAZORLA
WALCOTT
HAZARD
OSCAR
MPARD
NALD
XAVI
MATA
ETO'O
MAR JR
NI
CAVANI
IBRAHIMOVIĆ
MESSI
A. INIESTA
ISCO
BALE
RONALDO
BENZEMA
HIGUAIN

Fans of Ukrainian club, Shakhtar Donetsk turn a stand black and orange with their club scarves during a 2013 league match. The fans had a great season as Shakhtar won the league championship and the Ukrainian Cup.

SHAKHTAR-DONETSK

⚽ Some merchandise can be very strange. Hull City sold a toilet seat in their black and gold colours when the club reached the 2014 FA Cup final. MLS club, San Jose Earthquakes, sell clay heads of their striker, Steven Lenhart, in which fans can plant seeds that grow to form the player's long hair. Italian club, Fiorentina, even sold cans of air taken from their stadium.

THAILAND

A market stall in Thailand displays a range of shirts carrying the names of global football stars, most of whom play for the biggest clubs in Europe.

CRAZY FANS

Football fans care about their team, but some fans are absolutely football crazy. These fanatical fans go further than most. One example is Jan van Kook, a fan of Dutch club, Feyenoord. He bought two tickets for all the home games one season – one for him and one for his dog!

Fans' passion can get the better of them. In 2005, after a seven-year battle in the courts, a Colombian football fan was allowed to change his name to the club he supports, calling himself, Deportivo Independiente Medellin Giraldo Zuluaga! In 2015, a Norwegian-Liverpool couple named their baby daughter YNWA – short for 'You'll Never Walk Alone', the song sung by Liverpool fans.

SWEDISH FANS

Swedish fans have fun in skintight suits coloured like their country's flag before a crucial Euro 2012 match in Kiev. The 'Blue-Yellows' are known for their good humour and turning up at major tournaments in large numbers.

Graffiti from Boca Juniors fans in Buenos Aires. When attacker, Carlos Tevez rejoined Boca, his childhood club, in July 2015, over 40,000 Boca fans turned out at the club's stadium to greet him.

BUENOS AIRES

This mad-keen Irish fan with a beard dyed to look like his country's flag was just one of over 20,000 Republic of Ireland supporters who travelled to Poznan in Poland for Ireland's Euro 2012 match versus Croatia.

IRISH FAN

"I'M A SOCCER SLAVE. I DRINK FOOTBALL, I EAT FOOTBALL, I TALK FOOTBALL. EVERYTHING IN MY LIFE REVOLVES AROUND SOCCER. IT IS MY PASSION."
SADAAM MAAKE, SOUTH AFRICAN FOOTBALL FAN

CHANTS AROUND THE WORLD

Fans love to sing together and every team's fans have a number of different songs and chants they sing. Here are a selection of commonly sung chants and songs from different countries of the world.

HUP HOLLAND HUP

"Go Holland Go / Don't let yourself be stripped of your vest / Go Holland Go / Don't put slippers on the beast / Go Holland Go / Stay undaunted / Because a lion in football boots / Can beat the whole world."

SLOVENIA

"Kdor ne ska e ni slovenec!"
"He who is not jumping is not Slovenian, hey hey hey!"

SPAIN

"Andrés Iniesta, Vamonos de fiesta!"
"Andrés Iniesta, Let's go party."
After the Spanish midfielder, Andres Iniesta, scored the goal that won Spain the 2010 World Cup.

NUMBERS GAME
114
The number of years that fans of Norwich City have chanted their song, 'On The Ball City'. It is believed to be the oldest football song still sung by fans.

CZECH REPUBLIC

"My Chceme Gol!"
"Give us a goal!"

BRAZIL

"Sou brasileiro, com muito orgulho, com muito amor."
"I'm Brazilian, with a lot of pride and a lot of love."

CHILE

"Vamos. Vamos Chilenos, esta noche, tenemos que ganar."
"Let's go Chileans, tonight, we have to win."

MALAYSIA

"Kami turun ke stadium sehati sejiwa."
"We went down to the stadium, One heart one soul."

CLUB CORNER

"Arise and sing for the tigers (players) of FC Liaoning"
FC Liaoning fans, China

"Carefree, wherever we maybe, We are the famous SKC."
Sporting Kansas City fans, USA

"Come on boys, make some noise, We're a team of class and poise, And our Adelaide is rolling along."
Adelaide United, Australia

"Ore no Tokyo, hokori o mochi! Tachi agatte minna de utaou!"
"We have pride in Tokyo! Everybody sing together!"
Fans of Japanese club, FC Tokyo

DUTCH FANS

Fans of the Netherlands football team are known as 'Oranje' for their bright orange colours. Here, they form a giant, noisy wall as they chant during a European Championship match. One of their most frequently sung songs is 'Hup Holland Hup' ('Go Holland Go').

FUNNY FOOTBALL CHANTS

Football fans often enjoy humorous jokes and chants aimed at themselves, the fans of the opposing team or, sometimes, the referee when he or she makes decisions they do not agree with.

SEONGNAM FANS

"Merciful Seongnam FC, How merciful they are! They could have scored 7 but scored only 3, How merciful they are!" Sung by Seongnam FC fans during K-League games in South Korea when they are winning well.

BARCELONA FANS

"Blaugrana al vent un crit valent tenim un nom el sap tothom: Barça, Barça, Baaarça!"
"Blue and claret blowing in the wind, One valiant cry, We've got a name that everyone knows: Barça, Barça, Baaarça!"

BOCA JUNIOR FANS

"River, tell me how it feels to have played in the second division? That stain will never be erased!" Boca Junior fans taunting their fierce rivals, River Plate, who were relegated to the Argentinean second division for the first time in 2011.

Some rival fans find it funny that Barcelona had a deadly serious hymn called 'Cant del Barça' composed for the club's 75th anniversary. It was first performed in 1974 by a 3,500 person choir and is now sung on the terraces by fans.

Some countries and clubs take chants very seriously. In 2015, MLS team New York City FC gave out chant sheets to all their fans so they could learn lots of new songs. Nine years earlier in the UK, the job of Chant Laureate was formed for a season with an amateur poet, Jonny Hurst, employed to tour English grounds and write new chants.

HULK

"Green in a minute, he's going green in a minute!"
Arsenal fans singing about Porto's striker, Hulk, during a UEFA Champions League match.

SCOTTISH FANS

BRAZILIAN FANS

"He has the hands of a lettuce!"
Chant of fans of Brazilian clubs when a goalkeeper fumbles a ball or lets in an easy goal.

"Deep fry your pizzas, we're gonna deep fry your pizzas!"
Scotland fans, taking the mickey out of themselves and their love of fried food, sung as a jokey warning to Italy's supporters during a World Cup qualifying match.

GOOD FUN FANS

Fans can be bright, colourful and noisy. They can be passionate and loyal, following their team whatever the result. For all their rivalry with opposing supporters, almost all fans are fun, friendly and keen to help out others.

From giving directions to the ground to helping someone who doesn't speak the language, fans frequently aid others. In 2013, Irish fans raised money to buy tickets for two young Austrian fans who lost theirs in Dublin. In 2015, Spartak Moscow's oldest fan, Otto Fisher was robbed. Other Spartak fans started a collection online and thousands of pounds were donated to the 102 year old.

AMAZING COSTUMES

Some fans like to stand out in the crowd and wear outrageous costumes as this fan of the Spanish national team wearing a superhero outfit illustrates. Spain fans have had a lot to cheer about in recent years with their side becoming World Cup champions in 2010 as well as winning Euro 2012.

CROATIA FANS

A Croatia fan poses for a photo before an important World Cup game. Supporters of differing teams regularly mix with each other at major tournaments, comparing their football experiences and enjoying friendly arguments over players and teams.

Many football fans raise money for charity or lead charity schemes to help make other people's lives better. Founded by football fan Gordon Hartman, the San Antonio Scorpions football club's entire profits are given to special needs charities.

Fans of Ukrainian club, FC Volyn Lutsk, wrap up warm to withstand sub-zero temperatures on the open terraces of their snow-covered ground. Fans brave all weathers to turn up and support their team.

NUMBERS GAME

6,525,072

The number of pounds raised by Soccer Aid 2014, a charity football match held in Manchester featuring teams of celebrities and footballers including Alessandro Del Piero and Andriy Shevchenko.

"WE'RE TRYING TO HARNESS THE PASSION OF FOOTBALL FANS TO MAKE A DIFFERENCE."

JON BURNS, FOUNDER OF LIONSRAW, WHICH LEADS FOOTBALL FAN VOLUNTEERS TO BUILD COMMUNITY PROJECTS IN POOR COUNTRIES

1. Which club sold 945,000 replica football shirts in 2014: Kaizer Chiefs, Bayern Munich or AC Milan?

2. Which country's national team fans often clean up their litter after a match?

3. Which famous English club was previously known as Newton Heath?

4. To which Italian club did Benfica sell an eagle to be their mascot?

5. Who or what did Feyenoord fan Jan van Kook buy a second season ticket for to accompany him on his team's home matches?

6. Can you name either of the two teams that contest the Cairo derby?

7. Which Italian club sold cans of air taken from inside its stadium?

8. What sort of creature was Fuleco, the mascot of the 2014 World Cup?

WEBSITES AND BOOKS

http://www.stadiumguide.com/figures-and-statistics/lists/europes-highest-attendances/
This website lists the top 100 teams by how many fans attend each of their home games.

http://www.thebesteleven.com/2009/08/mls-and-usl-soccer-mascots.html
Check out photos of 25 of the best mascots in MLS and USL football in the United States.

http://www.bbc.co.uk/sport/0/football/29242557
Details and pictures of five of the world's greatest football derbies.

Truth or Busted: Football
by Adam Sutherland (Wayland, 2014)

Radar Top Jobs: Being a Professional Footballer
by Sarah Levete (Wayland, 2013)

Football Joke Book
by Clive Gifford (Wayland, 2013)

GLOSSARY

AFC Champions League
A competition for the leading clubs of each country in Asia held every year.

African Cup of Nations
The tournament for the best national teams in Africa.

A League
The top football league competition in Australia, contested each season by ten teams.

attendance
The number of people who watch a particular football match.

Bundesliga
The German league championship competition.

dugout
The covered bench and seats sat on by a coach, his or her staff and the team's substitutes during a game.

FIFA
Short for the Fédération Internationale de Football Association, the organisation that runs world football.

merchandise
All sorts of objects and clothing branded in the colours or logos of a football club or national football team.

MLS
Short for Major League Soccer, it is the top league competition for clubs in the USA and Canada.

professional
Someone who is paid for playing a sport.

relegated
To drop out of one league division and to play the next season in a lower division.

season ticket
A ticket which allows a fan to go to all of a team's home games throughout a season.

Serie A
The top division of the Italian football league.

UEFA
Short for the Union of European Football Associations, the organisation that runs football in Europe.

ANSWERS

1. Bayern Munich
2. Japan
3. Manchester United
4. Lazio
5. His dog
6. Zamalek, Al-Ahly
7. Fiorentina
8. An armadillo

INDEX

The publisher would like to thank the following for their kind permission to reproduce their photographs:
Key: (t) top; (c) centre; (b) bottom; (l) left; (r) right
All images **Dreamstime.com** unless otherwise indicated.
1 (b) iStock. com; 10 (bl) Graeme Maclean; 12 (bl) Benutzer:Elwedritsch.